GRANDMOTHER'S MEMORIES

A KEEPSAKE JOURNAL

This journal was given with gratitude to my grandmother

____

by her loving grandchild(ren)

____

A SPECIAL NOTE TO GRANDCHILDREN

Grandmothers are simply the best. It's a well-known fact. No one gives better hugs, brighter smiles, or more helpful advice. (And cookies, if you are lucky.) So how do you let your grandmother know how much you really appreciate her? One way is by giving her this special memory journal. There are prompts on its pages to help her tell her story, from the upper branches of her family tree all the way down to you. You will find out secrets, learn about family traditions, and appreciate what makes your grandmother such a treasure. You can read the journal together and ask even more questions about your grandmother's life and your place in a loving family. The memories and wisdom that your grandmother will share will make a wonderful and unique keepsake for you. The greatest gift a grandmother gives is her love, and each page will remind you of that. We sincerely hope you will enjoy giving and receiving this journal.

CONTENTS

MY FAMILY TREE

My Great-Grandmother

My Great-Grandmother

My Great-Grandfather

My Great-Grandfather

My Grandmother

My Grandfather

My Mother

Me

My Sibling

My Sibling

My Great-Grandmother

My Great-Grandmother

My Great-Grandfather

My Great-Grandfather

My Grandmother

My Grandfather

My Father

My Sibling

My Sibling

My Sibling

Chapter One
OUR
FAMILY STORY
LOOK BACK, LEARN, AND LOVE

A FAMILY BEGINS

Our family names are ____

____

____

____

Here's what I know about our family names: ______________________

____

____

____

____

Our relatives came from ______________________________________

____

____

____

____

I learned about them through ____

____

____

____

____

Some traditions we followed as a family were ___________________________

____

____

____

____

Here is an amazing story from our family's history: ____________________

____

____

____

____

*We are the accumulation of
the dreams of generations.*

STEPHEN ROBERT KUTA

YOUR
GREAT-GREATS

My grandparents were named _______________________

____

____

But I called them _______________________________

____

____

This is my own grandmother's story: _________________

____

____

____

____

____

____

____

My other grandparent has a story, too: _______________________________

____

____

____

____

____

This is how they met, where they lived, and what they did: _______________

____

____

____

____

____

____

A great-grandparent's heart
is a patchwork of love.

UNKNOWN

Something I'd like to tell you about my grandmother is _______________

____

____

____

____

____

____

Words I would use to describe my other grandparent: _______________

____

____

____

____

Things I remember the most about my grandparents: _________________

____

Ways you remind me of them: _________________________________

YOUR GREATS

My parents were named ____

____

____

But I called them ____

____

____

My brothers and sisters were ____

____

____

This is my mother's story: ____

____

____

____

____

This is my other parent's history: ____________________________

____

____

____

____

They met when ____

____

____

____

The places they lived were ____________________________________

____

____

____

*If nothing is going well,
call your grandmother.*

ITALIAN PROVERB

My parents' jobs were ________________________________

____

And ____

____

But they really enjoyed doing __________________________

____

And ____

____

Here's what our family life was like: __________________

____

____

____

____

____

____

One thing our family loved to do together was _______________________________

____

____

What I'd like you to know about my mother: _______________________________

____

____

What I want to share about my other parent: _______________________________

____

____

____

The things they passed down to me were _______________________________

____

____

A memory to share from when I was your age: _______________________________

____

____

____

WHEN I
WAS BORN

I was born on _______________________________

____

The day of the week was _______________________

____

In a place called _____________________________

____

____

My full name is _______________________________

____

My parents chose it because ___________________

____

____

____

____

As a baby I was ____

____

____

____

____

____

Here are the people who lived with us, and their dates of birth: ____________

____

____

____

____

____

____

____

Every house needs a grandmother in it.

LOUISA MAY ALCOTT

Chapter Two

ALL ABOUT ME

MY STORY TO SHARE WITH YOU

WHERE THE HEART IS

The place I lived when I was a little girl was _______________________

____

____

____

____

My first memories of home were _______________________________

____

____

____

____

____

____

Let me tell you about my room: _______________________________________

____

____

____

____

We had pets named ____

____

____

____

Something yummy we ate together was _________________________________

____

____

____

____

Home is people, not a place. If you go back there after the people are gone, then all you can see is what is not there anymore.

ROBIN HOBB

The friends I played with were ________________________

____

____

____

My favorite things to do were ________________________

____

____

____

I loved going to the ________________________________

____

____

____

The best place to hide was ________________________

____

____

____

Here is a story from when I was little: _______________________

____

STARTING SCHOOL

My first day at school was ______________________________

____

____

____

The school was called ______________________________

____

____

____

Here's how I got there: ______________________________

____

____

____

My first teacher was called ________________________________

____

____

____

____

My favorite school outfit was ____________________________

____

____

____

____

And I always carried ____________________________________

____

____

____

____

You're off to great places! Today is your day. Your mountain is waiting, so get on your way.

DR. SEUSS

Memories from my earliest years at school:

MOVING UP

I started middle school in _______________________________

____

____

____

My school was named _______________________________

____

____

____

The subjects I liked learning were _______________________

____

____

____

____

And the ones I didn't like so much were ______________________________

____

____

____

____

Everybody said I was good at ____

____

____

____

____

My best friends were ____

____

____

____

____

If you imagine it, you can achieve it. If you can dream it, you can become it.

WILLIAM ARTHUR WARD

Let me tell you some stories from this time:

SCHOOL'S OUT

The things I liked to do after school were ___________________

____

____

____

____

____

My hobbies were _______________________________________

____

____

____

____

____

When I was naughty and when I was nice: ______________________________

____

____

____

____

The best snacks were ____

____

____

____

My after-school friends were named ______________________________

____

____

____

CAMILLA EYRING KIMBALL

Weekends were special because _______________________

____

____

____

____

During winter breaks I used to _______________________

____

____

____

____

I looked forward to summer vacation because _______________________

____

____

____

____

My best vacation was ______________________________

____

____

____

____

____

____

____

This is how I loved to spend my ideal day out of school: ______________________________

____

____

____

____

____

HELLO, HIGH SCHOOL

I went to high school at ________________________

____

____

The subjects I enjoyed most were ________________

____

____

____

I spent a lot of time watching the clock in this class: ______

____

____

My friends were ______________________________

____

____

____

We liked to ____

____

____

____

My school activities included ____

____

____

____

My favorite after-school snack was ____

____

____

My go-to outfit for school ____

____

____

____

High school is about finding out who you are, because that's more important than trying to be someone else.

NICK JONAS

Here's how I would describe myself during
my high school years:

MY TIME AS A TEENAGER

When I was a teenager, I was crazy about ________________________________

____

____

____

My favorite kind of music was ______________________________________

____

____

____

I used to listen to it on my ____

____

____

____

An instrument I learned how to play: _______________________

____

____

____

____

The songs that spoke to me as a teenager: _______________

____

____

____

____

Musicians I loved and went to see were _________________

____

____

____

____

*It takes courage to grow up and
become who you really are.*

E.E. CUMMINGS

The best books and authors were ____________________________

____

____

____

____

My favorite character from a book was ________________________

____

____

____

____

Some of the movies I loved were __________________________

____

____

____

____

My favorite movie theater snack _______________________________

____

____

____

____

My favorite television shows were _____________________________

____

____

____

____

I never, ever missed an episode of ____________________________

____

____

____

____

My best friends were _______________________________

____

____

____

____

Like most teenagers, we used to wear _______________

____

____

____

____

One thing I will never wear again is _______________

____

____

____

____

How I wore my hair: _______________________________________

____

____

____

____

The things we thought were cool were _______________________

____

____

____

____

____

But definitely not ____

____

____

____

____

My favorite way to spend time was ________________________

____

____

I had jobs like ____

____

____

Someone who had a big influence on me was ________________

____

Because ____

____

____

If you met me as a teenager, you would see ________________

____

____

The bravest thing I did was ___________________________

____

____

____

Here's a secret your parents might not even know about me: ___________________________

____

____

____

____

Here's something important I learned when I was a teenager: ___________________________

____

____

____

____

HIGHER LEARNING

I went to college at ____

____

____

____

I chose this college because ____

____

____

____

____

My college tuition at the time cost ____

____

____

____

I went to school to study ____

____

____

____

____

____

____

I got a degree in ____

____

____

____

____

____

*Some people get an education
without going to college.
The rest get it after they get out.*

MARK TWAIN

My best friends in college were __________________________

One of my most memorable experiences was ____________________

Something I learned about myself I didn't know: _______________

Advice I would give you about going to college: _______________

Chapter Three

MAKING
MEMORIES

LIFE ON MY OWN

ON MY WAY

Here's what I did after finishing school: _______________________

____

____

____

____

____

My new home was in _______________________________________

____

____

____

____

____

The things that were important to me were _______________________

____

____

____

____

____

The hopes and wishes I had for the future were _______________

____

____

____

____

____

____

*You'll miss the person you are now
at this time and this place, because you'll
never be this way ever again.*

AZAR NAFISI

How I stayed in touch with my parents: _______________

____

____

____

____

The first thing I did when returning to my childhood home was _______________

____

____

____

____

How living on my own helped me to understand my family better: _______________

____

____

____

____

Here's something I learned from that time to share with you: ________________

____

____

____

____

____

____

____

____

____

____

____

____

CLIMBING THE LADDER

My first grown-up job was _______________________________

____

____

____

This is what I did: ______________________________________

____

____

____

____

____

This is how much I made a week or a month: _______________

____

____

____

Some of the best things about the job were ________________________

____

____

____

____

____

____

____

But to be honest I could have done without the ________________________

____

____

____

____

____

*A new job is like a blank book
and you are the author.*

UNKNOWN

Every job is a learning experience, and I found out that

The next jobs I held were

One job that I will never forget was

What I was really hoping to do was _______________________

____

____

____

____

____

____

If I could go back and change something about that time, it would be _______________

____

____

____

____

____

____

MAKING A HOME

How I felt making my own home for the first time: ______________________

____

____

____

Where I lived was ____

____

____

How much my rent or mortgage was: ______________________________________

____

____

The view from my window was ____

____

____

My favorite room was

Something I brought from my parents' house was

A keepsake I still have from that time is

Some of the other places I lived were

I started to feel like a grown-up when

The ache for home lives in all of us.

MAYA ANGELOU

GOOD TIMES

Here's how I loved to spend my free time: ______________________

____

____

____

Would you find me outdoors or in? ______________________________

____

My social life was ____

____

____

____

Good friends included ____

____

____

____

The places I loved to visit were ___________________________

____

____

____

My top three movies were _______________________________

____

____

____

Three favorite songs I played on repeat: ___________________

____

____

____

Bet you didn't know I could dance the ____________________

____

____

____

*Happiness comes out of being willing
to do your work in your twenties,
to find out who you are, what you love.*

CANDACE BUSHNELL

I never left home without ______________________________

____

____

____

My go-to weekend outfit was ______________________________

____

____

____

And one I'd rather not be seen in now was ______________________________

____

____

____

I got around by ______________________________

____

____

____

Something new I tried or learned was ______________________________

____

____

____

____

____

____

____

No weekend was complete without ______________________________

____

____

____

____

____

LOVE IS
ALL YOU NEED

Where and when I first met my partner/spouse: _______________________

____

____

The first thing I noticed was _____________________________________

____

____

____

____

Here's the true story of how we met: ________________________________

____

____

____

____

____

Our very first date was ____

____

____

____

____

____

There was a second date because ___________________________________

____

____

____

We dated for ____

____

*The best thing to hold onto
in life is each other.*

AUDREY HEPBURN

The most fun we had together was _______________________

____

____

____

____

____

____

____

One time I'd rather forget was _______________________

____

____

____

____

____

____

When I first met my partner's/spouse's family _______________________

____

____

____

____

The moment I fell in love: ____

____

____

____

____

How we committed to each other: __________________________________

____

____

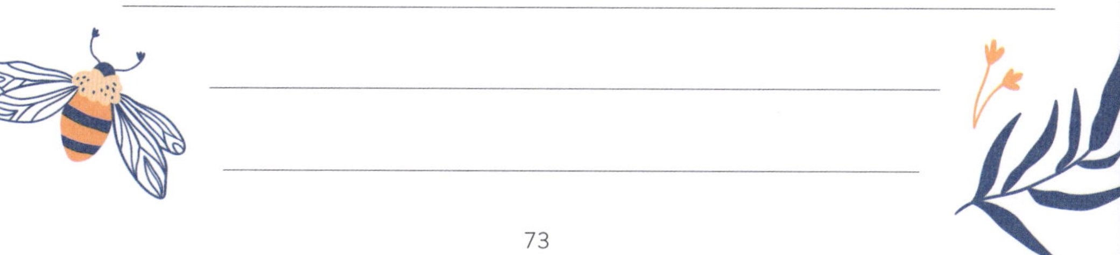

____

____

TYING THE KNOT

Where and when we made it official: _______________________

____

____

____

Some of our guests were _______________________________

____

____

____

Let me tell you about what we wore: _____________________

____

____

____

____

The things I will remember forever about that day are _______________________________

____

____

____

____

Something funny also happened that day: _______________________________

____

____

____

Our hopes and dreams for a life together were _______________________________

____

____

____

*True love stands by
each other's side on good days,
and stands closer on bad days.*

UNKNOWN

A LIFE TOGETHER

How our life together began: _______________________________

____

____

Our first home together was _______________________________

____

____

We were best friends with _________________________________

____

____

____

Some of the things we liked to do were _____________________

____

____

____

How being together changed me: _______________________

____

____

____

____

Here is a story from that special time: _______________

____

____

____

____

____

____

____

____

To love is nothing. To be loved is something. But to be loved by the person you love is everything.

UNKNOWN

Chapter Four

TIMES TO TREASURE

WELCOMING YOUR PARENT TO THE WORLD

HELLO, BABY!

When I found out I was pregnant with your parent I felt ___________________

____

____

____

We were living at ____

____

We welcomed your parent at ____

____

____

The first time we saw your parent we __________________________________

____

____

____

Here's a little bit more about the day your parent was born: ______________________

____

____

____

____

We named your parent ____

____

Because ____

____

____

____

And your parent's nickname was ____

____

____

We never know the love of a parent
till we become parents ourselves.

HENRY WARD BEECHER

My memories of your parent as a tiny baby:

STARTING TO GROW

How I would describe your parent as a young child: _______________________

____

____

____

____

Other people in your parent's family, before and after, were _______________

____

____

____

____

A person who looked after your parent was _______________________________

____

____

____

Who your parent looked like: _______________________________

____

____

____

What my parents had to say about your parent: _______________

____

____

____

____

Let me tell you how I felt as a new mother: _________________

____

____

____

____

This is a place where grandmothers hold babies
on their laps under the stars and whisper
in their ears that the lights in the sky
are holes in the floor of heaven.

RICK BRAGG

Stories, songs, and books your parent loved are

____

____

____

____

An activity your parent never got enough of was _______________________

____

____

____

____

Places your parent loved to go: _______________________

____

____

____

Favorite games were _______________________

____

____

____

Foods your parent found yummy were ________________________________

____

____

____

____

The best toys were ____

____

____

____

____

Your parent could not go to sleep without _______________________

____

____

____

____

____

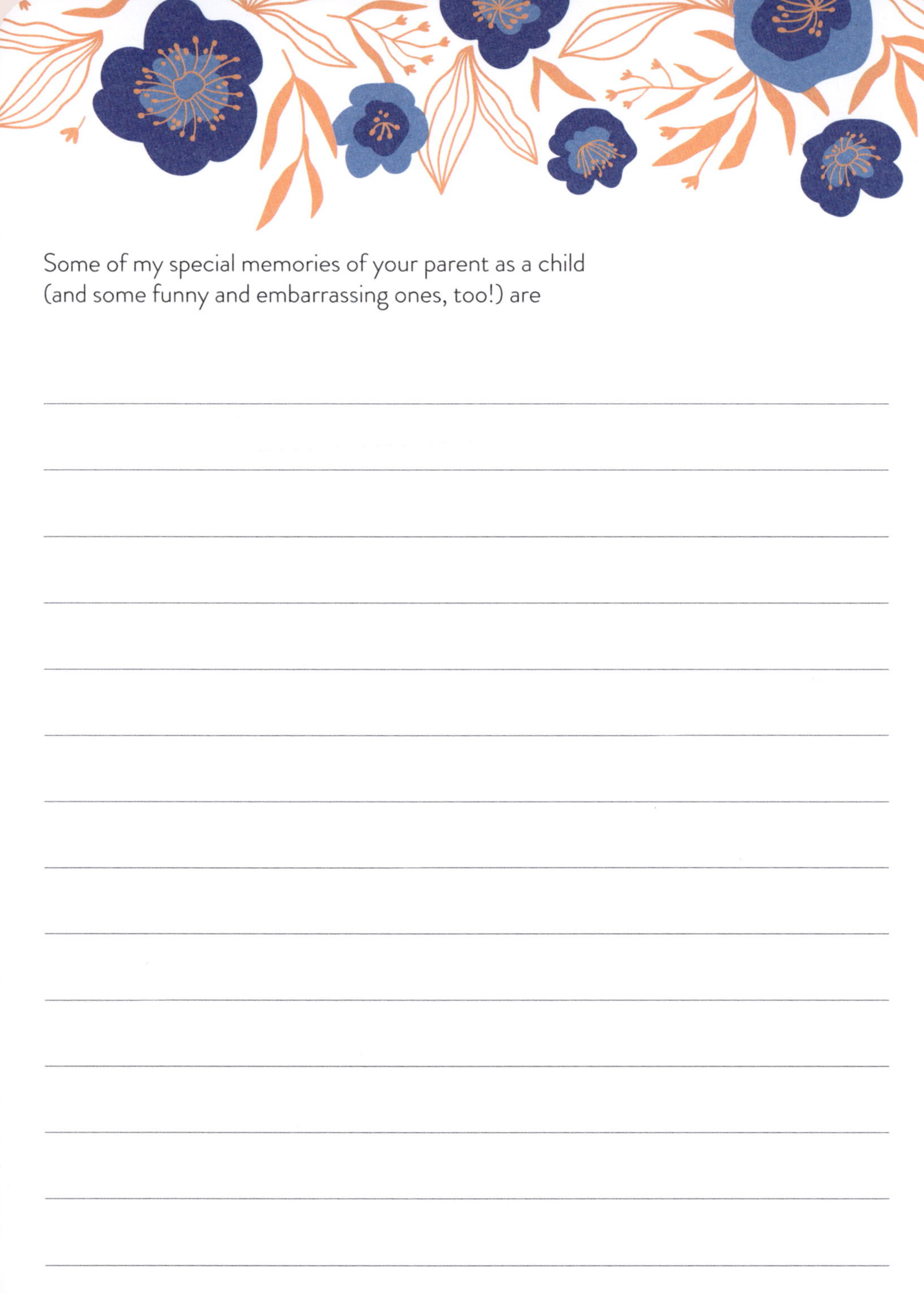

Some of my special memories of your parent as a child
(and some funny and embarrassing ones, too!) are

READY
FOR SCHOOL

Your parent's first school was _______________________________________

____

Here's how I remember the first day: ___________________________

____

____

____

____

____

Your parent got to school by ___________________________________

____

____

After school, your parent always _______________________________

____

____

Sports, clubs, and hobbies your parent was involved in:

____

____

____

____

____

____

Let me tell you about your parent's report cards in those early years:

____

____

____

____

____

____

____

Education is what remains after one has forgotten what one has learned in school.

ALBERT EINSTEIN

GROWING UP

Your parent went to middle school at ________________

____

____

What your parent liked about school was ________________

____

____

____

____

Something that was not so popular was ________________

____

____

____

____

____

After school, you could find your parent ___________________________________

____

____

____

I remember a funny story from that time: _______________________________

____

____

____

Your parent's best friend was ____

____

____

____

____

Dreams come a size too big so
that we can grow into them.

JOSIE BISSETT

FAMILY FUN

The things we always did as a family included _______________________

____

____

____

____

Our favorite weekends together always had _______________________

____

____

____

____

The pets we had were _______________________

____

____

____

During the summer, we would ______________________

____

____

____

Here's how your parent got along with the rest of the family: ______________

____

____

____

Let me tell you a funny story your parent will never share: ______________

____

____

____

____

*Home is where you are loved
the most and act the worst.*

MARJORIE PAY HINCKLEY

TEEN TIMES

As a teenager, your parent couldn't get enough of ___________________________

____

____

Your parent liked to wear ____

____

____

The music coming through the bedroom door was usually _______________

____

____

And let me describe that bedroom: ___________________________________

____

____

____

____

Your parent made me proud when ______________________________

____

____

____

____

____

But I was a little annoyed when ______________________________

____

____

____

Your parent's personality was like yours in this way: ______________

____

____

____

____

It's difficult to decide whether
growing pains are something
teenagers have or are.

UNKNOWN

Let me tell you all about your parent's experience in high school:

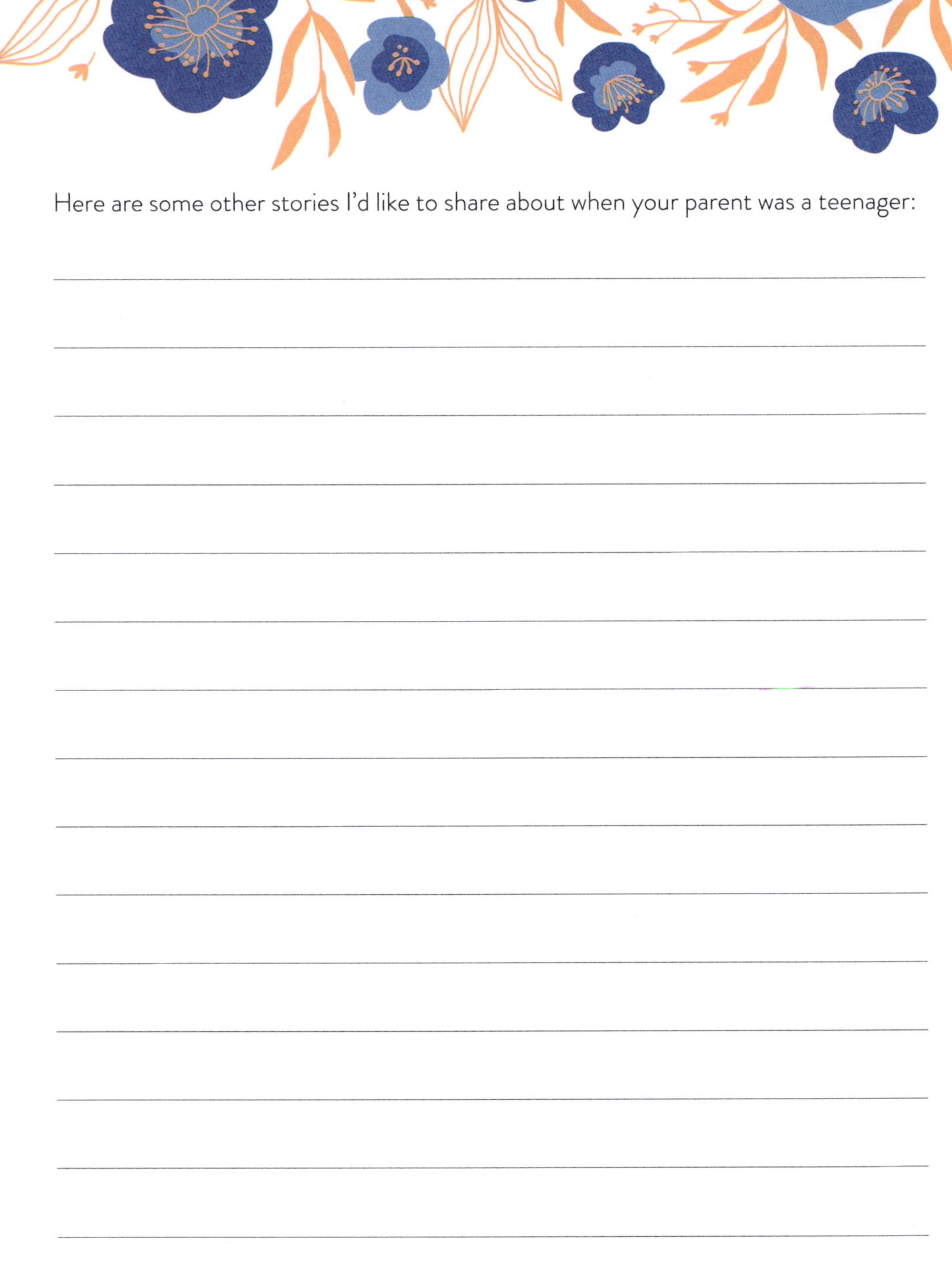

Here are some other stories I'd like to share about when your parent was a teenager:

FLYING
THE NEST

Your parent's dream for the future after school was _______________

____

____

____

What your parent did and where: _______________

____

____

____

Here is what I remember about the first time your parent left home: _______________

____

____

____

____

What I missed the most was ___________________________

____

____

____

____

Something I didn't really miss was ___________________

____

____

____

____

I knew your parent was really growing up when _______________

____

____

____

____

Leaving home's a cinch. It's the staying,
once you've found it, that takes courage.

CATHERINE WATSON

YOUR PARENTS MEET

Your parents met at ____

____

____

____

Here's what happened the first time I met your other parent: ____________

____

____

____

____

What surprised me was ____

____

____

____

____

I thought this might be a special relationship when ______________

____

____

____

____

Let me tell you a story from the time your parents met: ______________

____

____

____

____

____

____

____

A simple hello could lead
to a million things.

UNKNOWN

Here are my memories about when your parents
decided to make a life with each other:

BIG NEWS

When I found out you were going to be born, I ___________________________

____

____

____

____

____

This is how I got the news: ____

____

____

____

____

____

____

When you appeared, I was _______________________________

____

____

____

This is how I first met you: _________________________

____

____

____

____

I couldn't help feeling _______________________________

____

____

____

____

*I used to think I was too old
to fall in love again, then
I became a grandparent.*

UNKNOWN

Chapter Five

FROM ME TO YOU

BECOMING YOUR GRANDMOTHER

WELCOME TO THE FAMILY

My memories of your first few months are ________________________

____

____

____

____

____

____

____

____

____

____

This is how your mother was: _______________________________

____

____

This is how your other parent was: _________________________

____

____

A funny question about babies they had for me was ___________

____

____

____

This is what it felt like to hold you: _________________________

____

____

____

Children are the rainbow of life.
Grandchildren are the pot of gold.

IRISH BLESSING

YOU REMIND ME

You were grandchild number __________________________________

____

The family member you reminded me of is ____________________

____

Because ____

____

____

____

I think you looked like __________________________________

____

Because ____

____

____

Here are the ways you remind me of your own parent: ______________________

____

____

____

____

____

____

____

____

____

____

*Grandchildren are the dots
that connect the lines
from generation to generation.*

LOIS WYSE

YOU AS A BABY

This is how I would describe you as a baby: ________________________

____

____

____

____

Everyone else in the family thought ________________________

____

____

____

____

One thing that made your own personality shine through was

One of the best memories from that time is

Just when you think you know all that love is, along come the grandchildren.

UNKNOWN

YOUR PARENTS
AS PARENTS

These are the things your mother loved about having a baby:

And your other parent felt

If they came to me about advice, it was ______________________________

____

____

____

____

____

____

____

____

____

____

____

There are places in the heart you don't even know exist until you love a child.

ANNE LAMOTT

ME AS A GRANDMOTHER

This is how I felt about becoming a grandmother: ________________________

____

____

____

____

____

This is what surprised me the most: ___________________________

____

____

____

____

____

A special gift I gave you when you were tiny was _______________________

____

I chose it because ____

____

____

____

Things I learned as a grandmother, to pass on to you: ________________

____

____

____

____

____

____

A garden of love grows in a grandmother's heart.

UNKNOWN

This is a place to collect special memories
between just you and me:

MY HOPES AND DREAMS

After you appeared in our family life, I wanted the most wonderful future for you.
This is what I was thinking about:

A grandmother is a little bit parent, a little bit teacher, and a little bit best friend.

UNKNOWN

Chapter Six

OUR TRADITIONS

THE RITUALS AND RECIPES
THAT MAKE US A FAMILY

FAMILY HERITAGE

Our family's nationality is _______________________________

____

____

____

Our ethnic background is _______________________________

____

____

____

____

Here are some of the places your ancestors came from: ________

____

____

____

____

Some traditions we followed from our ethnic heritage were ___________________

____

____

____

We also followed these religious traditions: _________________________________

____

____

____

They are important to us because ____

____

____

____

*In all of us there is a hunger . . . to know who
we are and where we have come from.*

ALEX HALEY

GATHERING
TOGETHER

Our shared family beliefs include ______________________

____

____

____

____

Some of the holiday traditions we follow include ______________________

____

____

____

____

____

____

The holidays that have always meant the most to our family have been

____

____

____

____

____

Our family usually gets together when ___________________________

____

____

____

____

____

____

A family is a little world
created by love.

UNKNOWN

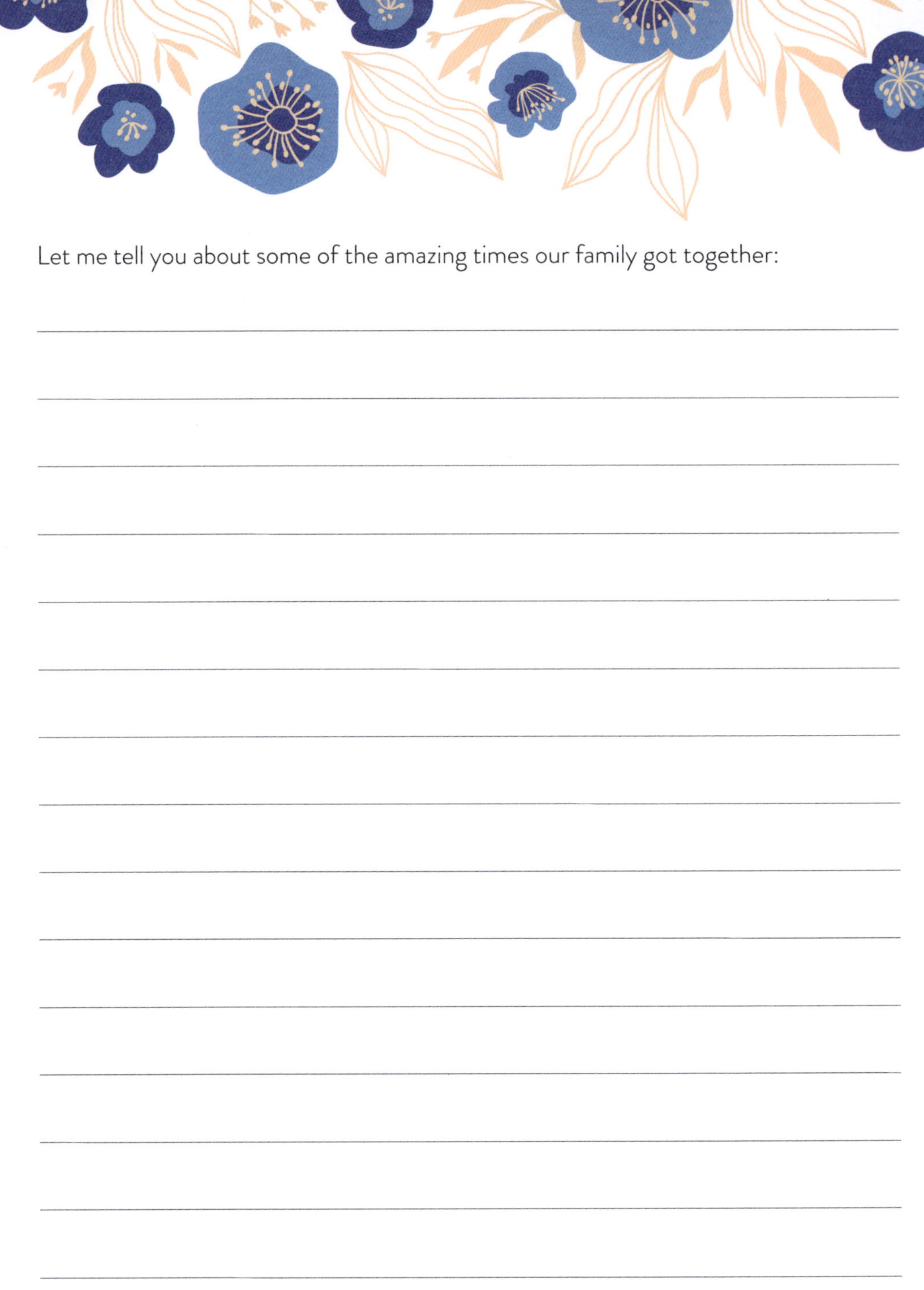

Let me tell you about some of the amazing times our family got together:

FOOD FOR THOUGHT

Traditional family dishes that we ate were ______________________

____

____

____

Something I remember about family meals when growing up: ______________________

____

____

____

____

Our family had rules about dinnertime: ______________________

____

____

____

____

Some of the foods we ate on special occasions were ___________________

____

____

____

____

Here are some family members and their special dishes: ___________________

____

____

____

____

____

____

____

____

____

*Memories are made when
gathered around the table.*

UNKNOWN

FAMILY RECIPES

Here are some of the family recipes we've loved to make and eat over the years:

Recipe: ____

Ingredients:

_______________________   _______________________

_______________________   _______________________

_______________________   _______________________

Instructions: _____________________________________

____

____

____

____

____

____

Recipe: ____

Ingredients:

_________________________________   _________________________________

_________________________________   _________________________________

_________________________________   _________________________________

_________________________________   _________________________________

Instructions: ____

____

____

____

____

____

____

____

____

There's just so much love that
goes into home cooking.

MING-NA WEN

SPECIAL HOLIDAY RECIPES

On holidays and special times, you could always find on the table:

Recipe: ____

Ingredients:

_______________________   _______________________

_______________________   _______________________

_______________________   _______________________

_______________________   _______________________

Instructions: _______________________________________

____

____

____

____

____

____

____

Recipe: ____

Ingredients:

Instructions: ____

MY RECIPE FOR HAPPINESS

Just for you, here is grandmother's recipe for happiness:

Recipe: ____

Ingredients:

_________________________   _________________________

_________________________   _________________________

_________________________   _________________________

_________________________   _________________________

Instructions: ____

____

____

____

____

____

____

Recipe: ____

Ingredients:

_______________________________   _______________________________

_______________________________   _______________________________

_______________________________   _______________________________

_______________________________   _______________________________

Instructions: ____

____

____

____

____

____

____

____

Know your worth.
Believe, tolerate, and allow.

UNKNOWN

Bluestreak

An imprint of Weldon Owen International.

www.weldonowen.com

ISBN: 978-1-68188-641-1

PRINTED IN CHINA

10 9 8 7 6 5 4 3

Grandmother's Treasures

Use these pages to capture the memories, stories, or significance of the treasures and keepsakes you chose to store in your box.

THE TREASURED KEEPSAKES OF

____

Description:

The story about this keepsake:

Description:

The story about this keepsake:

Description: ________________________________

____

____

The story about this keepsake: ___________________

Description: ____

____

____

The story about this keepsake: _______________________

____

____

____

____

____

____

____

____

____

____

____

Description: _______________________________

____

____

The story about this keepsake: _______________

____

____

____

____

____

____

____

____

____

____

____

Description: ____

____

____

The story about this keepsake: _______________________

Description: ____

____

____

The story about this keepsake: ________________________

____

____

____

____

____

____

____

____

____

____

____

Description:

The story about this keepsake:

Description: ____________________________________

____

____

The story about this keepsake: _______________

____

____

____

____

____

____

____

____

____

____

____

Description: ______________________________

____

____

The story about this keepsake: __________________

____

____

____

____

____

____

____

____

____

____

Description:

The story about this keepsake:

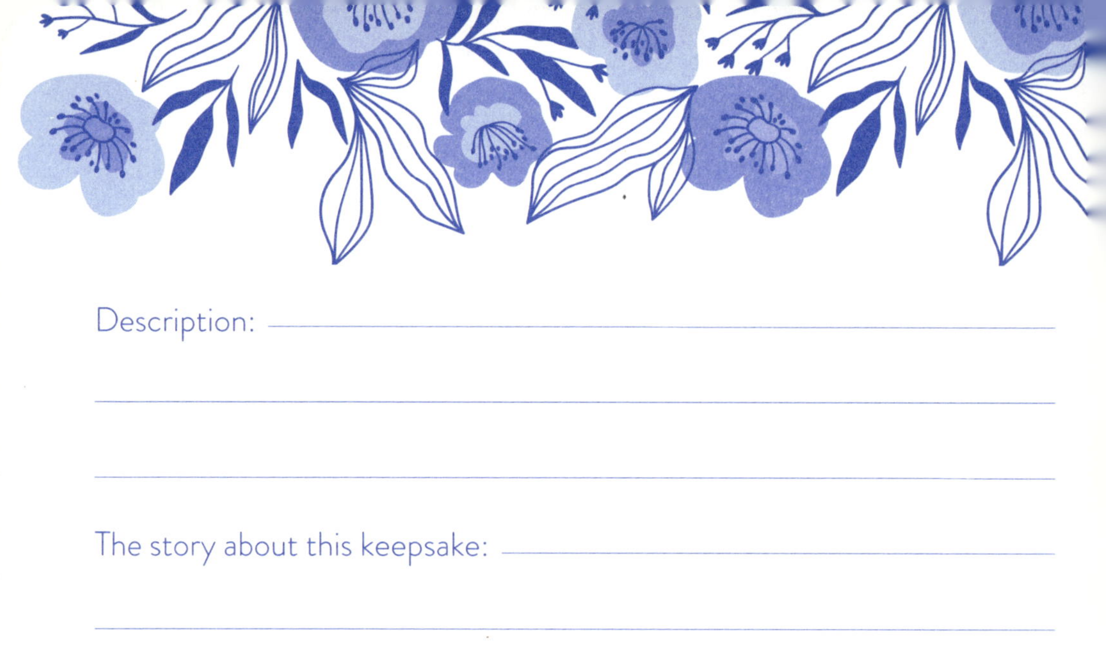

Description: _______________________________

____

____

The story about this keepsake: _______________

____

____

____

____

____

____

____

____

____

Description:

The story about this keepsake:

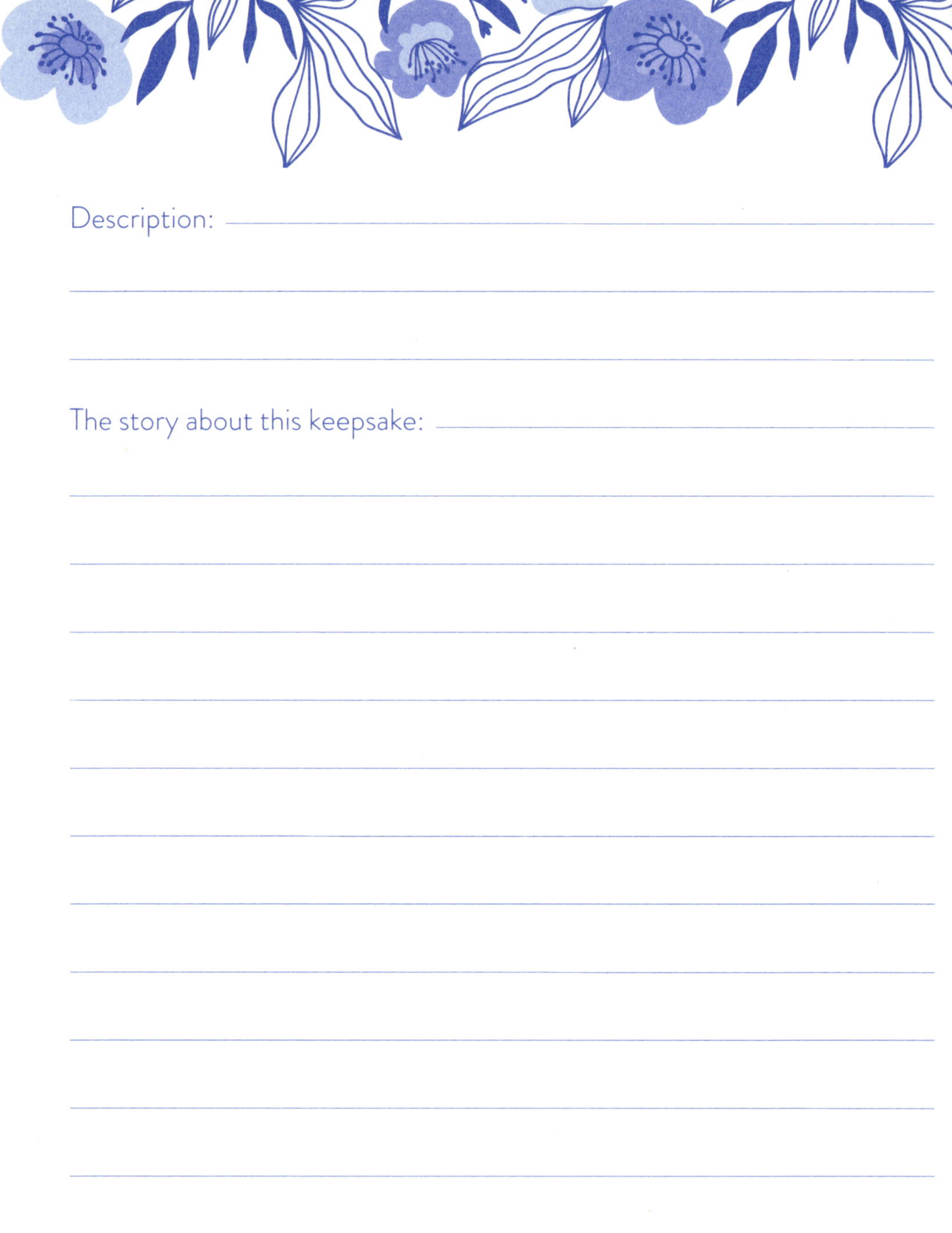

Description: ________________________________

____

____

The story about this keepsake: ________________

____

____

____

____

____

____

____

____

____

____

Description:

The story about this keepsake:

Bluestreak
BOOKS

An imprint of Weldon Owen International.

weldonowen
www.weldonowen.com

© 2022 Weldon Owen International.
All rights reserved.

Printed in China

3 4 5 6 7 8 9 10